FINDING PEACE
AT
WORK AND HOME

A Workbook to Track and Change How Your Home and Work Lives Interact

CHRISTOPHER L. SMITH

DEDICATION

This workbook is dedicated to each person who wants to value themselves as a whole person. May they each be guided on their journey to achieve balance between the different parts of their life, especially between their home life and their work life.

INTRODUCTION

❝A man should never neglect his family for business.
Walt Disney

❝'No' is a complete sentence. It does not require justification or explanation.

❝I don't think you're as capable of handling lack of sleep or whatever challenges you throw at your body as you get older.
Bill Gates

What happens at home can change how we are when we get to work. Certainly, anyone who has a new baby in their house will have an understanding of this. However, an argument with a family member can put us in a mood all day or have us worrying about what we will face when we get home.

If we are honest with ourselves, there are also times that problems we have encountered at work play out once we get home. You have to behave in certain ways when you are interacting with customers and coworkers but the frustrations keep building up. Finally, when you are safely at home, it can all come out.

Learning how these two parts of our lives interact is the first step in getting better overall peace and wholeness for ourselves. Once things have been identified, then you can begin working on making changes to break the bad habits you have. This will allow you to value both your work and your home life.

Having a therapist or counselor can be helpful in order to talk about what is going on, to help point out things that might be going on under the surface and to encourage alternative ways of handling what is going on. This book is not meant to be a substitute for such guidance, in fact this book can be helpful for recording what is going on so that you and your therapist or counselor can more clearly work with what is going on. Our memories of events can get fuzzy so writing things down at the time can really help. It can be especially helpful to keep track of these things every day.

Even if you do not have a therapist or counselor, going through the exercise of recording what is going on and thinking about it can be helpful. This book gives you the opportunity to do just this. Each entry in this book will allow you to use two facing pages to track what is going on for a particular day. On each log, you will be asked about what took place, your thoughts and feelings about it, what you did, the result and any changes you would make next time. As you do so, watch for patterns and see if you are able to move more to responses over time.

Think about why you picked up this book. How has your work been impacted by your home life? Who at home has been bearing the brunt of things you have brought home from work or perhaps as the result of staying over at work? Write down some of your thoughts.

_____

_____

_____

_____

_____

_____

_____

_____

_____

_____

_____

_____

_____

_____

What happened at home before I went to work (including how I slept):

What happened at work today:

How I felt when these things happened:

How I felt about myself and my day when I left work:

What happened at home after work:	How I felt about what happened and myself:

Connections I see between work and home:

What I will try to do differently another day:

What happened at home before I went to work (including how I slept):

What happened at work today:

How I felt when these things happened:

How I felt about myself and my day when I left work:

What happened at home after work:	How I felt about what happened and myself:

Connections I see between work and home:

What I will try to do differently another day:

What happened at home before I went to work (including how I slept):

What happened at work today:

How I felt when these things happened:

How I felt about myself and my day when I left work:

What happened at home after work:	How I felt about what happened and myself:

Connections I see between work and home:

_____

_____

_____

_____

What I will try to do differently another day:

_____

_____

What happened at home before I went to work (including how I slept):

What happened at work today:	How I felt when these things happened:

How I felt about myself and my day when I left work:

What happened at home after work:	How I felt about what happened and myself:

Connections I see between work and home:

What I will try to do differently another day:

What happened at home before I went to work (including how I slept):

What happened at work today:

How I felt when these things happened:

How I felt about myself and my day when I left work:

What happened at home after work:	How I felt about what happened and myself:

Connections I see between work and home:

What I will try to do differently another day:

What happened at home before I went to work (including how I slept):

What happened at work today:	How I felt when these things happened:

How I felt about myself and my day when I left work:

What happened at home after work:	How I felt about what happened and myself:

Connections I see between work and home:

What I will try to do differently another day:

What happened at home before I went to work (including how I slept):

What happened at work today:

How I felt when these things happened:

How I felt about myself and my day when I left work:

What happened at home after work:	How I felt about what happened and myself:

Connections I see between work and home:

_____

_____

_____

_____

What I will try to do differently another day:

_____

_____

_____

What happened at home before I went to work (including how I slept):

What happened at work today:	How I felt when these things happened:

How I felt about myself and my day when I left work:

What happened at home after work:	How I felt about what happened and myself:

Connections I see between work and home:

What I will try to do differently another day:

What happened at home before I went to work (including how I slept):

_____

_____

_____

What happened at work today:	How I felt when these things happened:

How I felt about myself and my day when I left work:

_____

_____

_____

What happened at home after work:	How I felt about what happened and myself:

Connections I see between work and home:

What I will try to do differently another day:

What happened at home before I went to work (including how I slept):

_____

_____

_____

What happened at work today:	How I felt when these things happened:

How I felt about myself and my day when I left work:

_____

_____

_____

What happened at home after work:	How I felt about what happened and myself:

Connections I see between work and home:

What I will try to do differently another day:

What happened at home before I went to work (including how I slept):

_____

_____

_____

What happened at work today:	How I felt when these things happened:

How I felt about myself and my day when I left work:

_____

_____

_____

What happened at home after work:	How I felt about what happened and myself:

Connections I see between work and home:

What I will try to do differently another day:

What happened at home before I went to work (including how I slept):

_____

_____

_____

What happened at work today:	How I felt when these things happened:

How I felt about myself and my day when I left work:

_____

_____

_____

What happened at home after work:	How I felt about what happened and myself:

Connections I see between work and home:

What I will try to do differently another day:

What happened at home before I went to work (including how I slept):

What happened at work today:

How I felt when these things happened:

How I felt about myself and my day when I left work:

What happened at home after work:	How I felt about what happened and myself:

Connections I see between work and home:

What I will try to do differently another day:

What happened at home before I went to work (including how I slept):

What happened at work today:

How I felt when these things happened:

How I felt about myself and my day when I left work:

What happened at home after work:	How I felt about what happened and myself:

Connections I see between work and home:

What I will try to do differently another day:

What happened at home before I went to work (including how I slept):

_____

_____

_____

What happened at work today:	How I felt when these things happened:

How I felt about myself and my day when I left work:

_____

_____

_____

What happened at home after work:	How I felt about what happened and myself:

Connections I see between work and home:

What I will try to do differently another day:

What happened at home before I went to work (including how I slept):

_____

_____

_____

What happened at work today:	How I felt when these things happened:

How I felt about myself and my day when I left work:

_____

_____

_____

What happened at home after work:	How I felt about what happened and myself:

Connections I see between work and home:

What I will try to do differently another day:

What happened at home before I went to work (including how I slept):

_____

_____

_____

What happened at work today:	How I felt when these things happened:

How I felt about myself and my day when I left work:

_____

_____

_____

What happened at home after work:	How I felt about what happened and myself:

Connections I see between work and home:

What I will try to do differently another day:

What happened at home before I went to work (including how I slept):

What happened at work today:	How I felt when these things happened:

How I felt about myself and my day when I left work:

What happened at home after work:	How I felt about what happened and myself:

Connections I see between work and home:

What I will try to do differently another day:

What happened at home before I went to work (including how I slept):

What happened at work today:	How I felt when these things happened:

How I felt about myself and my day when I left work:

What happened at home after work:	How I felt about what happened and myself:

Connections I see between work and home:

What I will try to do differently another day:

What happened at home before I went to work (including how I slept):

What happened at work today:

How I felt when these things happened:

How I felt about myself and my day when I left work:

What happened at home after work:	How I felt about what happened and myself:

Connections I see between work and home:

What I will try to do differently another day:

What happened at home before I went to work (including how I slept):

_____

_____

_____

What happened at work today:	How I felt when these things happened:

How I felt about myself and my day when I left work:

_____

_____

_____

What happened at home after work:	How I felt about what happened and myself:

Connections I see between work and home:

What I will try to do differently another day:

What happened at home before I went to work (including how I slept):

What happened at work today:

How I felt when these things happened:

How I felt about myself and my day when I left work:

What happened at home after work:	How I felt about what happened and myself:

Connections I see between work and home:

What I will try to do differently another day:

What happened at home before I went to work (including how I slept):

_____

_____

_____

What happened at work today:	How I felt when these things happened:

How I felt about myself and my day when I left work:

_____

_____

_____

What happened at home after work:	How I felt about what happened and myself:

Connections I see between work and home:

What I will try to do differently another day:

What happened at home before I went to work (including how I slept):

What happened at work today:

How I felt when these things happened:

How I felt about myself and my day when I left work:

What happened at home after work:	How I felt about what happened and myself:

Connections I see between work and home:

What I will try to do differently another day:

What happened at home before I went to work (including how I slept):

_____

_____

_____

What happened at work today:	How I felt when these things happened:

How I felt about myself and my day when I left work:

_____

_____

_____

What happened at home after work:	How I felt about what happened and myself:

Connections I see between work and home:

What I will try to do differently another day:

CONCLUSIONS

By now, you should have a better understanding of how and why these two important dimensions of your life interact. You may have ideas of how to reestablish balance between them and may even have made great progress towards this. As you work on this, you will realize that you are developing better control over your life. Hopefully, with this you will be experiencing more wholeness and peace (or shalom) in your life.

It is possible to establish wholeness and peace in your life. Remember what is contained in the words of Koi Fresco:

   ❝   Balance is the key to everything. What we do, think, say, eat, feel, they all require awareness, and through this awareness we can grow.

If you are still having difficulty establishing this balance, you might want to find a counselor or therapist that you can trust and sit down with them. They have methods that can help you explore what is going on and look at alternatives.

ABOUT THE AUTHOR

Of course, in the truest sense of the word, you and those part of your journey are the author of this journal. However, the framework has been created and produced for you by the one listed as the author, Christopher L. Smith.

Christopher has been involved in a diverse range of areas in his training and experience. His approach through life is not to treat these as distinct dimensions, but rather to see the connections across various dimensions. This book blends together his training in pastoral counseling that began at Yale Divinity School with the organizational structures learned studying operations research.

His own work with clients, at the time of preparing this resource, was through Seeking Shalom (www.SeekingShalom.org), a teaching practice in New York and Indiana of which he is the founder and clinical director, where clinicians intentionally incorporate spirituality into the therapeutic process. His professional life has also included service as the chair of the Presbyterian Serious Mental Illness Network and as the president of the American College of Counselors, as well as regional and local leadership roles. He is licensed as a marriage and family therapist, mental health counselor and clinical addictions counselor. His therapeutic work includes working with individuals, couples, families and groups around a variety of clinical issues.

In addition to this resource, Christopher has authored a number of other resources and books. If you are interested in learning more about his writings, please look him up at http://AnAuthor.com/Christopher.

www.ingramcontent.com/pod-product-compliance
Lightning Source LLC
Chambersburg PA
CBHW071640040426